WHOSE IDEA
WAS THIS?

ALS AS MY NEW NORMAL

Holly Ladd

Additional copies of this book may be ordered through Amazon,
Barnes and Noble, and other online retailers.

Whose Idea Was This?/ Holly Ladd. -- 1st ed.
ISBN 978-1-5120809-2-6

To Joan and Mike, with love

CONTENTS

Introduction

Holly Ladd died on June 23, 2014, in Newton, Massachusetts. She was 59 years old. Three weeks after her ALS diagnosis, she had already reviewed the prognostic literature, and, in her lawyerly fashion, constructed her advanced directive with clear limits. Then, over the next two years — the happiest of her life, in some ways — she pushed the limits back again and again.

Life before the diagnosis was full of high-power activism: heading the Boston Fair Housing Commission, helping to found the Boston AIDS Consortium, traveling through Africa teaching health providers to use state-of-the-art technology. She volunteered for the local Red Cross, running out to scenes of fires and floods. There was an emotional toughness ("you could hear her eyes roll," said a friend), and a certainty that she knew many, if not all, answers. She kept her heart apart for her personal life: her partner, their son, a few nephews and their children, a few close friends, and her beagle-basset hound Walker, who had separation anxiety.

Life after the diagnosis was involuntary adjustment and softening. First, she couldn't walk. "I don't want to live in a wheelchair," she said — but did. Then she couldn't use her hands. "If I can't feed myself, I don't want to live," she said — but did. With each loss, her capacities shrunk, but her desire for life grew, and she expanded what she was willing to lose. She who had roamed Africa couldn't go to the bathroom alone anymore.

Gestures of generosity towards Holly, the ones that arrive with acute illness and recede as illness becomes chronic, did not recede. Over time, they only increased. More and more people visited, and more often. Her nephew installed ramps in his house so she could come for Christmas dinner. Her son moved back to town so he could drop by every morning at 8 and lift her out of bed. Kids sat on her moving bed, charmed, and learned to use her eye-gazer computer. The source of her imprisonment was the source of their magic.

All the unremitting love astonished her. Before she lost the ability to speak, she recorded hundreds of messages that she could pull up on the computer with her eyes.

Some were full of gratitude, some bantering, some about golf ("are you still hitting them wild to the right?" her voice would ask). There were also commands for Walker the dog, whose separation anxiety had been fully treated by her constant presence.

Blinking once or twice to clarify, she kept pushing back the directives of when she wished to die. This amazed those around her. But she was bowled over by love, absolutely bowled over, and didn't want to miss a thing.

Elissa Ely, MD
Remembrance Project
WBUR

Month One – We Got Through It

Dear friends –

- Month One is in the books. We got through it. Nothing much has changed except everything.

- Crisis. "You have got to be f*#king kidding me!!"

- After months of searching for a cause for my weakening legs and constant reassurance from all doctors that I did not have ALS – I have ALS.

- The news was devastating and left Joan and me stunned in bed for a Saturday morning stuck between disbelief and the urge to action – but what to do?? Gather data, tell people who need to know, assess resources, and survey the infrastructure and plan. In short, we are in crisis mode.

- The Telling Phase – god awful as each time it feels like it becomes more real. Enough – from now on, please just tell whomever you want. I don't want to have to tell anyone else.

- I am reading a book – co-written by Barbara Okun, my new therapist – "Saying Goodbye: A Guide to Coping with a Loved One's Terminal Illness." I highly recommend it. In it the authors revisit and recast the Kubler-Ross five stages of grief to reflect the changes in medical care and technology over the past forty years. Since living with and dying from diseases now is a much longer and more drawn out process, the Kubler-Ross analysis needed an update. Stage one is Crisis. We are there. Stage two is Unity – and we are moving there with all of you.

What we know and have done to date:

- We have a diagnosis. We know that there is no cure and that everyone's experience of the disease process is different within some general parameters. (Look it up, I am not repeating it all here – none of it is good.) So far it seems that only my legs are symptomatic but I do have occasional nerve twitchings in my back. I have to use a walker, which I have been doing since August, now however I have to get a more serious unit. I also have a new leg and foot brace for my left leg to keep me from dragging that foot. But all in all, I am happy that this stays in the legs.

- I have my medical team in place at the Fenway and BI, and have engaged the folks at the clinical trial program at MGH. I have my regular physical therapy and as mentioned above a very good mental health provider.

- We are working with Tim, Rick and Donna on the modifications to the house and hope to start the construction very soon.

- I have engaged lawyers and financial people to make sure all the insurance and investments are set and that we redo how we handle our money to make sure critical bills are paid and that Joan has access to my funds. The health proxy is in place.

- Work is cool with all this for now, my local staff is terrific and have gone out of their way to ensure that I have a comfortable work space and can get in and out of the building safely. Travel to DC is still the norm, but maybe not for too much longer. My boss and my colleagues at FHI could not be more supportive.

Becoming a PALS (person with ALS):

- This is the hardest part. We talk about it constantly. I am part of a "community" I did not choose. A self-definition I reject. A patient. A consumer. An ill person. A burden.

- When your doctors call you to find out how you are doing, you know that you are toast. I am doing fine, my heart is broken.

- So we will meet with the rep from the ALS Association and Compassionate Care ALS, and Walter from the PALS lunch at BI and all the other services to assess my needs, our needs and eligibility for assistance. Review the best and worst of the care providers, compare walkers, wheelchairs and vans…

- More than I can take at the moment. I will have to take all this in small bites. I am crying more than I have since all my friends were dying of AIDS. I guess, with that experience, I have some better sense of what is to come and how one becomes the personification of the disease if not careful. I need to stay Holly for as long as I can.

What I have learned:

- Check your insurance policy documents, not just the summaries provided by your employer. While reading the fine print is tedious, you really don't want to be surprised. For instance, the long-term disability policy that I have through work does not supplement Social Security Disability payments; the insurer reduces the amount of the benefit by that amount. This seems unfair since I have paid for both. Also, if I draw down from my retirement account at work (employer contribution) they will also reduce the amount of the disability payment by that amount. Again, this seems grossly unfair since the retirement contribution was compensation for past years' work and "earned". As employees we don't have a say in the terms of the disability insurance, we take it or leave it and I suppose some benefit is better than no benefit. Still, I am just saying…

- Long Term Care – wow. Glad I did this. Glad I bought the inflation rider.

- Lawyers have not been the best use of money. Necessary, but you will get as much information online. Unless you have a lot of real estate or investments, you don't need fancy and you will save yourself time and money reading up on disability stuff on the web. Wills too, not much to think about – just leave it all to Joan and Mike and maybe leave some special wishes, but in the end leave it up to them what to do with everything.

- Advance directives, power of attorney and other paper. Just do it, you can always change your mind and redo. So maybe today I think no extraordinary measures, no ventilator. Six months ago I would have said no wheelchair.

- Medical care. Relationships matter. Women are smarter and spend more time with you. You have to drive the bus.

- Research – you are a subject – this is not about relationships.

- Friends (including Joan's family). The best.

What's Next:

- Unity – this is sort of like circling the wagons and expanding the network at the same time. The "Saying Goodbye" book really focuses on families of origin for its models. And, as you know, that is not really much of an option for me when looking for a care network. You have all stepped up in major ways this month, and there will be more and more to do as this progresses. As we come to terms with this new reality we will figure out what we need, and what roles there are to fill. It is as important – or maybe even more important – to support Joan through this since she will do most of the heavy lifting both emotionally and practically. And stay in touch with Mike, even if he does not call back.

- Hopefully the medical visits will slow down now so the schedule can be more predictable. I learned this week that I do not have breast cancer. Seriously, can we pile on anymore? There was actually a moment when I was called in for a third set of images (aka squeezes) where the technician said that we had to roll and squeeze the breast just so (ouch!) to get a 3D image of the "object"! Imagine my calculation as I am sitting alone in the waiting room trying to decide if it would be better to die of breast cancer or ALS – or if the treatment of the cancer would preclude me from participating in clinical trials for new ALS therapies.

- It was great to have Donna along for the nasty EMG test in August when Joan could not be there. Maybe we can do more of that going along thing. It is helpful to have folks around and would have made the debate about whether to treat the breast cancer more interesting!

- Not so good – having folks over on weeknights unless you bring dinner or we have take out. It was too much before this to have to prepare dinner on a work night; now it is just not possible as I am of no use for food prep or shopping.

- The dog. Sigh. He will take a walk with anyone so please, feel free to come by and take him. This is a great favor.

- Revisioning – Re vision. Revise. The house will go through some changes hopefully soon to make it easier for me now and to prepare for the future. I also need to sort out the closets and toys. I think I can let go of the clothes I have been saving for years on the chance that either I will once again fit in them or that I might need to dress up for work. So a fall chore will be a big Goodwill sort. I also need to sell my new bike and move all the golf equipment out. I won't use either; they take up room and are a sad reminder.

- The camera stuff also needs a hard sort. Once I get used to the new me, maybe I can get back to the camera. But maybe it will be a lighter kind of camera. In any event all the portrait studio equipment can go.

- And then the last big category of thinking is what to do about work. How long to keep working at FHI – an equation that must take into account income, health insurance and benefits versus time and energy and soul. As a person who has always worked, and to large degree drawn my identity from my work, it is hard to imagine not working. As much as I was also looking forward to retiring, which was to spend more time doing things that no longer seem realistic – a photography business, travel and golf. So this needs some thought.

More to come...

Month Two – Vulnerability and Appreciation

SUNDAY, OCTOBER 7, 2012

On being vulnerable (a ramble on the way to the monthly update):

I have lived my life, as much as possible, trying to avoid being vulnerable. I believe that most of us do this, some more focused on the physical and others maybe the emotional vulnerabilities. It is always a balance – adventure, travel, exploration, love, commitment, sharing and true friendship all require that you trade off some of the impregnable self. Vulnerability is not always a matter of choice or negotiation – being mugged on the city street, hurt as a child or lied to by those you trusted are not in our control. But generally speaking there is a lot of consciousness in the process of setting up boundaries.

Now this ALS – a whole new un-negotiated and unwelcomed sense of vulnerability. Exposed, unsafe, at risk. Like when walking on a city street with both hands glued tight to the walker, dodging cracks in the sidewalk that can send me flying, and totally open to the intentional and unintentional interference of those rushing (really, now, they are just walking) by me. I noticed that while my attention is so focused and my eyes are glued to the ground in front of me, I am easily startled by people coming up to me from behind. I hang off the side of the car inching my way from the back seat where I have tossed the walker to the driver's door hoping not to get sideswiped by a bike or a truck. Emotionally exposed, one glance at the airport can throw my whole composure to the floor. Imagine someone has to put your shoes back on after the security screening while you sit in the wheelchair trying to drive your feet into them. I need my friends, my doctor, my job and Joan so much and I am so afraid that they will all tire of this, of me.

I asked the kid from Compassionate Care ALS, when he came by the other night, when do I get to feel sorry for myself? He said "Not yet".

Too much to do:

There is still too much to do to let the ALS take over. Lots of appointments still, trying to get everything in place. Meetings this past week with the lawyer to wrap up the will, the clinical trial team at MGH to get involved in their research and donate some skin and blood to the cause. Then there was another doctor visit, mental health visit, and of course physical therapy. At home the carpenter was in for several days working on some new handrails for the central staircase so I can keep going up and down on my own. We are picking out tile for the first floor bathroom and making plans for the holidays.

I love my community, friends, the little things and politics (really):

The Red Sox let us down, and in the end they were not much of a diversion. Thank god we have politics. Ronnie has been over for the Mass. Senate debate and the first Presidential debate, which were both only slightly better than watching the Red Sox end the season being blown out by the Yankees. With five more debates before election day I should be able to amuse myself – I just hope I don't throw a shoe through the TV!

People are being incredibly kind and whether it is phone calls from Israel or coming over to fix my photo printer, I am only alone when I truly want to be.

Joan just brought me a freshly cooked piece of bacon! and then a second slice!! (little things!!!)

Mike came up from NY to celebrate Joan's birthday and to help with some of the change of season chores. The dog still literally falls at his feet.

Donna, Ellie and others have offered to help with chores and Adam and Diane take Walker for a walk most evenings (see dog below). Everyone checks in. I feel cared about, and while it makes me shy I admit that it feels very nice.

Golf gone:

We all have these fleeting moments. I know, they should make you smile recalling some special feeling. Like a quick breeze, you have a sensation or a memory out of the blue. Today somehow I had a breath of Bass River Golf Course. I gave Liz my golf clubs when she stopped by last weekend. Get over it.

Insurance fighting:

Nothing is as clear in fact as it seems in the brochure. I am still trying to convince the long term care people that I am definitely going to be unable to wash, feed, dress, toilet or otherwise care for myself without assistance very soon and that waiting until I actually need a wheelchair lift or roll in shower will be too late to start building these essential modifications to the house.

So, while there is money designated in the policy to modify the home to enable me to stay here (rather than a nursing home) I cannot yet access the funds. I am not bad enough yet. Like, hello? There is no other direction for this to go but down. No mystery here.

After multiple phone calls and letters they are finally agreeing to assess my functional status. At least I will have something from which to launch an appeal. Maybe if nothing else I have found a target for my anger.

Work (with a commentary on medical care):

I am trying to stay fully engaged at work, but it is hard. I have so many appointments out of the office and have used up all my vacation and sick time. I am trying to keep up. I am trying to make the benefit system work for me. I love my staff, I have a great team and I enjoy going to the office to see them. The DC team is very sensitive and eager to help.

I took what will surely be my last solo trip to DC. I went down on a Wednesday and came home on Thursday – or I should say came back to Boston on Thursday. I ran into trouble while in DC with what was probably just a major full trunk muscle spasm. This was incredibly painful and kept me awake all night in the hotel. I was short tempered and spent an uncomfortable Thursday in the DC office simply waiting to catch my flight home.

I arrived at Logan and we went to Newton only long enough to drop off the dog and then went right to the ER where I spent the next 12 hours waiting for a bed. Finally admitted on Friday morning I was surprised (relieved, grateful) to see my primary care doctor at the end of the bed ready to direct my care. I got home Saturday and have been surprised again about how long it takes to get your feet back under you.

So, I have been grounded by the neurologist. I can still drive to the office in Watertown. I can still work from home. People can fly up from DC. No more TSA!

The Dog:

People have come through for Walker (not to be confused with walker – the furniture I push around in front
of me everywhere I go). He is getting regular walks with
the upstairs dog, Bodee, and Ronnie and Donna are getting to be his new best friends (not sure that this is mu-
tual for them!). Lucky us! He is the cutest pain the butt.

Handing things over:

I cannot be in control of everything anymore. It is however, really important to hang on to what I can control
and be really clear with myself and others what those
are, and how it changes. I have to let other people do
things for me. So I am practicing with Joan's birthday,
fixing my photo printer, getting coffee at the office and
driving. I love to drive. I know that my driving days are
coming to an end, prolonged maybe by moving the gas
and breaking functions to the steering column. I am
practicing by asking for rides and learning to sit in the
passenger seat.

How do I feel?

All of this is beginning to set in. While most days I still
can't believe it is true, I am beginning to move past

shock. I am scared. I really do love my life and enjoy so much the sunny crisp days we have in the New England fall. I will find my balance, I know.

So far (please God) this has continued to stay in my legs, although I worry about my arms. I think the arms are just tired from hauling me around. And even though that is no easy job, the medical advice is to not try to lose weight. Imagine after all these years hearing that!

I notice that I am a lot more tired and that I tire much more quickly. I take longer to get things done and this extra effort is contributing to being tired. The neurologist says to start conserving my energy. I need to be able to get up and down stairs. I certainly need to be able to sleep in my own bedroom for as long as possible. My short-term goal is to get past Thanksgiving. New handrails on the staircase help a lot.

Book this month – "I Remember Running: The Year I Got Everything I Ever Wanted–and ALS," by Darcy Wakefield.

Month Now –
Diagnosis plus Three

SATURDAY, NOVEMBER 24, 2012

This month it is harder to write than I thought it would be. I guess it's because the living with ALS is getting harder, more real and I am less able to distract myself with organizing details. The reality of this disease, my new life, is settling in on me and I am afraid of what lies ahead. Big changes I know, but also the small ones that I am not so quick to notice until I see what I have already lost. Yet as much as I hate all of this, I see how I am blessed by a circle of strong and thoughtful friends who come to my side daily with kind words, support, a meal or just a laugh. We are all trying to come to terms with this unfairness that is changing all of us.

I know what this stage looks like as I prepare to move past it – the introduction of equipment to keep me doing as near the same daily routine that I have always done – walkers and seat lifts, bed rails and straps to grab and lift my legs. All these things to make it possible to continue as before getting up and out the door. True none of it easy and none of it without help. But the next phase I cannot bring myself to imagine. I have yet to find the manual to tell me how to live life from a wheelchair. From a wheelchair it is hard to pretend that I am "just a little weak." From a wheelchair it is hard to figure out how to stand up straight and tall and look people in the eye. From a wheelchair I don't know how to get out of the house. I can imagine how it will be to be bed ridden; I think that we have all seen that movie. But I don't know how to negotiate halfway between my life and no longer me.

[Margin note: People don't realize how important this is]

[Margin note: → What makes us, us? @ what point do we lose our sense of self? Notice the importance of meaningful @ccupations.]

News:

1. Finally the long-term care insurance people are willing to agree that I am sufficiently disabled to make me eligible for benefits. This means I can get help paying for the modifications to the house. These little "victories" are quite perverse.

2. I am leaving work at the end of the year (more about this below) and coming to terms with being "disabled" in that context is something else altogether. *dealing w/stigma new challenges + equipment definition of normal + self*

3. Construction is taking longer than planned – no surprise – but luckily I am still able to get upstairs (with considerable help) and can use the shower (again, with considerable help) so the delay in completing the first floor bathroom is something we can tolerate for a little while longer.

4. Pre-Thanksgiving (our annual dinner for 40 – 45 of our friends) went off this year without a hitch thanks to every one of our friends who stepped up to help on the day before, and stayed late to clean up Sunday night (and some smart menu choices by Joan!)

5. Thanksgiving in Chatham – all the New Jersey clan came up for the holiday so we could be together (we missed Cath who is studying in Scotland this year).

Weakness:

No more driving. I had an accident with the car a couple of weeks ago – a fender bender with only minor damage – and this has meant that I am no longer safe to drive. The truth is I could not recover quickly enough to avoid hitting the car in front of me when my foot slipped off the brake and hit the gas pedal. I can't take that kind of chance again.

It is getting much harder to walk, to get up and down stairs, in and out of the car and out of chairs. I struggled at the iParty store with the walker (the grown woman stacking the shelves actually asked if she could go for a ride on it!). I will need to start using a wheelchair soon. The wheelchair is such a symbol of defeat in my attempts to keep moving – to keep my legs moving – to be as independent as possible. I have a manual chair that I got from CCALS, but have yet to use it. Mike took it out of the car Thursday morning to make room for other stuff we needed to take with us for Thanksgiving. I cried watching him out the window. I am still having a very hard time seeing the chair as a tool for increased independence. It is a leg substitute.

But I walk so slowly and with such fear at times that I am drained and exhausted at the end of the day. Perhaps I will find that I have more energy if I give in to the chair. Perhaps also the weakness in my arms is from carrying myself and not from the ALS, in which case a wheelchair should relieve some of that as well. Perhaps I will find that I am still myself when being pushed from behind.

[handwritten margin notes:]

Something may seem small to you but have symbolic meaning. Symbol? to someone else.

Anatomy? Is it better to keep working your muscles though?

A combination of elements and circumstances has lead to the decision that it is time to leave work. I will go out on disability by Christmas assuming that my employer and I – and my doctor – can all come to terms. This is a great loss, I have always been the kind of person who defines myself by my work – I am a _____. Now I am a person with ALS who can no longer lead my team, travel to meet with my peers, my supervisors, and donors. I can no longer concentrate for a full day. I can no longer work every day from the office and work from home more days per week. I need help from my staff to get up from my desk. This week we are going to practice with the manual wheelchair to see if that is an easier way to be in the office.

→ You need an OT!

More to the point though, I am worried about how I fill my time, keep a sense of community, stave off depression and still be a part of the world. I have an invitation to volunteer at the Fenway Health Center's Research Institute. My friend Judy and I are working on an idea for a creative project, John will help me figure out how to keep taking photos and maybe I will find a way to put some energy into advocacy for access to ALS clinical trials and treatments in development.

(see www.treatusnow.org)

*Research idea maybe?
End of life occupations, making the most of the end of life.
Oh wow this could be a career!*

It is hard to lose something that defines you like grads, work, sport etc. I will put my potential in the Lord instead. That will take some of the tinker away

Winter promises to be a snowy one this year and if our first snow earlier this month was any test, I will find moving about a real challenge. That, combined with not driving makes the end of a regular work schedule a necessity.

Strengths:

- Humor. Somehow Joan and I are still finding things to laugh about. How klutzy can we be trying to get socks on!! A bit of denial perhaps, or maybe just protection.

- Friends. Our network is so strong and each person has reached into his or her own network to bring more resources. (Who knew that we would need occupational therapy skills – who knew that they were close at hand!)?

- Rides. As soon as I stopped driving people stepped up with offers to drive for me.

- Smarts. We are figuring this out as fast as we can. We are trying to stay one step ahead.

- Resources. Our own or borrowed – so far so good.

- Compassionate Care ALS. Who knew that this little organization was going to play such a big role in our lives? Please support them at www.ccals.org.

- Flexible health care providers. Both my therapist and my primary care doctor are now making home visits.

  → I watched the saddest video ever – so frustrated w/ health care system

- Joan and Mike. Mike really stepped up over the Thanksgiving break. What a sweet guy.

Plans:

- We are still trying to get the modifications finished on the house – bathroom is almost done but the ramp has not yet been started. When all that is done moving downstairs becomes an option.

- Cruise. Okay so it looks like we are taking a cruise in January – a seven-day pajama party in the Carib-bean with 5 or 7 other friends. A challenge for sure, could be lots of fun.

- A new relationship to work as a volunteer, a helper and no longer person in charge means a real oppor-tunity to think through what I really care about and where I can make a difference.

  take a person out of the position of dependent

- Study biology via the Kahn Academy (online) so I can understand the clinical research underway to treat ALS. → You Go Girl!

Make a difference – what is my legacy? I am inspired by how other people with ALS are spending their time. I need to get going. NO WHITE FLAGS!

December and
Happy New Year

MONDAY, DECEMBER 31, 2012

The end of the year is here. There will be no New Year's resolutions this year. This is now a day-to-day, week-to-week experience. I just want to live and stay mobile.

I turned 58 this month and enjoyed a quiet Christmas holiday at home with friends dropping by over the course of a couple days and dinner with Tim and his family in Winchester – he put in a temporary ramp to enable me to get in and out in one piece.

Bob built a similar set of platforms to get me into his and Donna's house for our annual Christmas dinner

Importance of Community

31

party. It is all in the willingness to try. Some things are too important to give up. Seeing friends for the most part requires them to come to me, and it is special to get out to see them in their own home.

Importance of environment on mental health

I stopped working in the middle of the month and it took me two days to realize that I need to start a project right away – or go nuts. I had enough on my to do list to get me through three days only. I can always start my taxes!

A home health aide starts here part time after New Years' Day to take over the morning assistance so Joan can refocus on work – and getting there on time. I am apprehensive about having a stranger around whose job is "me". In fact, there will be two women covering the week with me, alternating days. Each of these transitions is painful. They mark how the disease is moving ahead unchecked and how there really is nothing I can do to stop it or even slow it down. Something more to adjust to.

Speaking of adjusting, I can no longer climb the stairs to the second floor so we have rented "stair chairs" to cover the two parts of the staircase. So for now I ride. It was really good to know that these devices can be rented. To buy and install the system would have been nearly

$7,000. That would have been hard to justify if I only used it for a couple of months. Renting makes it possible to have the tools for the time required. I am using the manual wheelchair inside the house as a place to sit around in the rooms on the first floor. This makes it possible to use the whole downstairs, not just my one chair in the family room. For as long as possible, I still want to make the effort to live in the whole house. Some nights, though, getting upstairs is a real challenge.

What's next?

I will be getting a new "hospital" style adjustable bed. I have great difficulty getting into and out of bed, which I still have to do a few times each night. After a lot of thought I am going to spend the money and get a queen-size frame and use my own mattress. I just like being able to snuggle in bed or hang out there watching TV with friends. A single hospital bed, while covered by insurance, was just too sad a thing to cope with for the rest of my life. So this is a splurge – a bed from a company called Transfer Master in Iowa that will ship in the middle of January.

I also was fitted for my power wheelchair (a real monster of a machine). It should be ready at the end of January, once the insurance company approves the purchase.

I will next need to sell my car and buy a van to get around in. This is a very expensive disease.

The good –

Mike was a star over the holiday and even though he is coping with his own emotions around all of this, he was fully engaged and helpful, kind and patient. He and the dog have returned to Long Island for the month, giving Joan a break from daily dog care.

My ALS clinic visit this month was pretty routine. My hands are weaker but my lung function has improved. I can tell that my hands are weak – I have trouble opening things (water bottles, for example) and my handwriting is sloppy. My arms are hanging in, though, and I can still support myself on the walker.

I am being screened to be part of a clinical trial on a drug that might improve muscle function. I should know next week if I am going to be able to participate.

The construction is done, the bathroom is lovely and the ramp and path in the front of the house are just in time, enabling me to ride the scooter to the car.

My claims for short-term and long-term disability have both been approved. My separation agreement from work is done and they are being generous, all things considered. My long-term care insurance has kicked in and I can now get reimbursed for home-based support.

The not so good –

Joan fell and sprained her ankle the day before Christmas, a victim of trying to do too much. She is still trying to take care of me while limping painfully around the house. The good news is that she can use the stair chairs to get up and down the stairs.

Leaving work, getting a home health aide and buying all the new equipment continue the painful process of accepting this as my reality. There are days of great sadness, but not every day and not all day.

SNOW!!! This year it decides to snow. Crap.

I have decided that I have to sell the heavy Nikon camera and lenses that I have in favor of a lighter system that I can actually use. I think that might help get me back into photography. My big camera is sitting in the basket in the family room reminding me that I can't lift it.

This coming month –

The cruise – nothing ventured, nothing gained.

A clinical trial – fingers crossed.

Project one – working with a group of people impacted by ALS called Treat Us Now. This is a group advocating for access to drugs/treatments currently in clinical trial or not otherwise approved by the FDA on the grounds that because our condition is fatal, some of the development requirements put delays on our ability to try these drugs in time. This group reminds me of the early days of ACT-UP. What is missing are the things that made ACT-UP work – this is such a heterogeneous group of individuals with little if any advocacy or political background, who have very limited experience in being part of a self directed organization and whose egos and fear are all over the place. My goal is to help them get organized, and brave, without getting in too deep.

Project two – get back to taking pictures. Get a creative project underway with Judy that has a purpose and a "long tail".

Project three – get involved with the Fenway Institute as a volunteer.

Stay strong, send jokes.

Borrowing Faith

MONDAY, JANUARY 28, 2013

January – it is 2013. I can no longer say I was diagnosed "this year". When survival is measured in such small numbers, each year matters.

Can you borrow the faith of friends to carry you forward in the storm? I wonder.

I am not a religious or spiritual person. My parents had no particular faith or religious tradition and, although I tried on various colors and stripes, nothing stuck. I respect people who have a spiritual life, but have not been able to incorporate one.

Many friends and acquaintances have responded to the news of my ALS by saying that they are praying for me.

My reaction is always gratitude and, well, confused humility. If I don't believe, but they do, am I cheating by welcoming their prayers? Am I just "covering all the bases?" Does God care who is doing the heavy lifting? If you have faith but I don't, are your prayers wasted on me? Maybe by even asking the question I have betrayed my own skepticism. (Please feel free to reply with your thinking – let's have a conversation.)

Of course, Googled "borrowing the faith of others." Most of the hits had to do with borrowing money on faith; a couple were about how as we learn we borrow the faith traditions of our parents – but they also suggested that this was inadequate or "impotent" faith. One posting however offered a hint at what I am struggling with:

"When we go through a period of suffering, doubt can loom bigger than life, causing us to lose our focus on God, causing our faith to waver. It is during those times that we may need to "borrow" the faith of others to help us see clearly. For example, when my best friend was battling brain cancer, I could always tell when her faith was being shaken. I could hear it in her voice or see it in her worried expression. She was too weak and weary to focus on God, to stand firm in her faith, without help.

During those times, I would let her "borrow" my faith. I shared my eyes, eyes that were not clouded by tears, eyes that could still see a larger perspective, so that she could see God more clearly. I shared my heart, a heart not so badly bruised and battered by unanswered questions and broken dreams, so that she could feel God's presence near her. I shared my memory, a memory not altered by powerful winds of change, so that she could recall God's faithfulness. By sharing my faith, I could help my friend refocus her perspective and find peace."

(http://www.endurance.org/dealing-with-doubt-by-borrowing-faith)

So, to my friends who offer prayers on my behalf, please continue that special conversation. I will borrow your faith as I borrow Joan's strength and Debbie's humor and Donna's clear thinking and...

Resources revisited: A number of you have responded to my first post about the practical financial steps that I have taken in the past that are now providing benefits we could not do without. As I settle into my new life style, I am drawing on those resources now and it all seems to hold up. I have a new home health aide who spends 4 to 6 hours a day with me on weekdays. This is paid for by long-term care insurance. I have wrapped

If you lose employer-sponsored health benefits

up at work with an agreement for three months of short-term disability, COBRA benefits and my long-term disability will be kicking in come March. While I was able to reach a departure agreement that includes other cash and considerations that I very much appreciate the details are not disclose-able. But, suffice it to say we are okay. I have such good health insurance I will continue to use this (COBRA) as long as I can afford it before applying for Medicare.

If you are still thinking about buying extra insurance – just do it.

Medicine: Here is another test of faith – a leap of faith. It is irrational to think that my health care team can stop this disease, can save my life. But I do – or at least I wish it so much that I have leapt. I started on a clinical trial this month. This was huge – I felt that every day I was not on a trial was wasted. This drug should help me access my muscles. "Tirasemtiv selectively activates the fast skeletal muscle troponin complex and increases its sensitivity to calcium, resulting in increased skeletal muscle force and slowing of time to muscle fatigue."

Best case scenario – I get randomized to the drug and not the placebo, the drug works and at the end of the

trial the drug company lets me stay on it. But that is a lot
to hope for.
largest teaching hospital of Harvard Med. near Boston

I switched my care from Beth Israel to Mass General. It
just made sense to go where there were resources, na-
tional level expertise and a team that was dedicated to
beating ALS. I am borrowing their optimism. Like I
said, a leap of faith.

Friends, trust and love: Another investment of faith –
faith that my friends would take care of me. That was
hard given the task – get me on a plane to Florida, a
cruise in the Caribbean, and back on the plane home.
The anticipation of the endeavor literally kept me up all
night many times. So this was a lot of trust. My friends
came through and then some. While the plane was even
worse than I imagined, and it is pretty clear that flying is
out from here on, my friends held me for a week giving
Joan some free time and made sure I was safe and included in our week long pajama party. Let people get
your food, hold the elevators open, put your foot on the
right side of the scooter, push your wheelchair around
the ship, cut your food and – yes the most humbling –
clean you in the bathroom….. that is a lot of trust and a
lot of love. Just saying, thank you.

Of course it does not take a cruise. Love comes in a dinner left in the fridge, flowers left on the counter, a ride to a medical appointment, coming downstairs to fish the dropped remote control out from under my chair. I love you all.

This month coming: I am looking forward to volunteering at the Fenway Institute which should begin soon. I need to get my other projects back in motion, the transition month from work to retirement now over. I will be getting my motorized wheelchair this month and I will now need to sell my car and get a van that can accommodate the chair. I am joining the board of Compassionate Care ALS and the patient services committee of the local ALS Association. And of course there are tax filings to prepare. So I hope to stay busy, January had way too much daytime television.

More On
Borrowing Faith

FRIDAY, FEBRUARY 8, 2013

I have received many replies to the question about borrowing faith – some posted here and some sent by email to me. I am touched by both the number of you who have shared your own faith tradition/beliefs or your own struggle with the question of faith. A couple of friends responded that our life's work (or more precisely my work) is an expression of spirituality. I have trouble with that word – good does not equal spiritual. Challenged to think further, this is as far as I can get:

I think the right word is "grace". I know that I had a notion of karma – thinking if I spent my life doing good I would "earn" good — build some good karma. Good karma would keep bad things from happening. Now I see it does not work that way. Bad things happen. Grace is the ability to take on the bad things well, and karma is the gift of having people around who care and help.

That might be the best a nonbeliever with good karma can hope for.

That, and permission to call it a day when the courage is spent.

Howling at the Moon

SATURDAY, MARCH 16, 2013

I really appreciate all the thoughtful comments last month on borrowing the faith of others. I posted my summation (http://hollyladd.tumblr.com/post/42608786445/more-on-borrowing-faith) and invite you to read it and add further comment. I also encourage you to comment or ask questions as we go forward on this blog.

Time for a symptom update. I can no longer walk. I am no longer able to get out of a chair. I rely upon a mechanical device – a motorized lifting machine – to get me off of the bed or off of the toilet. I get wheeled across the house to the bedroom or to the wheelchair. My chairs have motors and so does my bed. I ride the ramp out the front door, and another to get off the front

47

porch and into the yard. Snow shoveling is critical to my safety, not just mobility.

I can no longer lift my arms above my shoulders. I can no longer open anything with my hands. I can no longer turn over onto my side in bed. There are a growing number of places I can no longer reach to scratch. I can no longer dress or undress myself. This will continue as I deteriorate.

I choke on food every now and then, and I speak more slowly. Both symptoms will intensify.

I can still type, talk and laugh. I can read and watch movies and TV. I can go for a ride in my new wheel-chair modified van. With help I can eat and drink – and enjoy vodka. I can think.

The drug trial continues but I am not able to tolerate a full dose of the experimental drug. It is having little or no effect on my symptoms.

Sorry to be so stark about my status, it has been a hard couple of weeks and it is important that we all get on the same page. ALS has no U-turns or exit ramps, and very few rest stops.

New This Month. I moved downstairs to the dining room. It got too dangerous to keep traveling up and down stairs; my legs are not strong enough to help get me up. Joan and I fell getting me out of the stair chair at the top of the stairs and had to call EMS to come help get me off the floor. Enough of that! We all could get hurt. I like the dining room with its bamboo wallpaper, multiple windows, morning sun and fireplace. I hate that I am here.

I've heard that around By Abilities Prob. Expo

My Permobil wheelchair now carries me everywhere I need to go. I am learning to use it. It is big and makes quite a statement. I keep banging into the furniture and doorframes. But yesterday I was able to go out and get a haircut, something I could not have done without the chair.

Later in March, Tim will use my scooter and we will race in a shopping mall and see who goes faster. After that I will most likely return the scooter to CCALS. They recently lent me a machine that we use to lift me out of a chair and move me to another seat. This device is a huge help for my caretakers. The "Molift" is a clever piece of technology made in Norway. It is far too expensive to own and I am once again grateful for the folks at CCALS for their help and extensive knowledge.

Goodbye red Toyota Venza. Hello Dodge Caravan. No style, a plain white mini van that has been reconfigured to enable me to drive the wheelchair in from the side door equipped with a ramp, turn around and pull into the space where the passenger seat normally sits. The thing serves its purpose. Liz stopped by this week on her way back to NY. We took the opportunity to run to iParty and trick the van out in tiki style – complete with an inflatable palm tree and a string of pink flamingo lights, bobble head monkeys and plastic drink cups. Much better!

I bought a big m....f.... honker of a TV last weekend to put in the dining room/bed room. Maggie urged, "go big" and I was able to take advantage of a sale. Adam unboxed it, and Timmy put it up on the wall. So now I can entice company to join me for the theater-like experience of life size baseball (or high def movies). "The Life of Pi" is startlingly beautiful on the giant 51" plasma screen!

I have started selling off camera lenses and will buy the new camera next week. I probably waited too long to do this. I need to figure out what I can hold and manipulate. Now that it is warming up and staying light longer I am eager to get out.

Beautiful movie, great book too.

I am working more with Compassionate Care ALS. I joined their board in February. They can use help as they quickly scale up. I also met with folks at the non-profit research organization ALS Therapy Development Institute, looking for a way to become more involved with them. I also attended the care services committee meeting with the Massachusetts Chapter of the ALS Association. I am not sure yet about this group.

Sometimes it might be just as hard on caregivers

And Others. Joan is hanging in; she and Mike are taking a brief respite this coming weekend – a well-deserved break. We are still somehow holding on to humor, re-marking at a 2 am bathroom run that we probably laugh more than any other couple dealing with this disease. And I guess that is the good news.

I continue to be surrounded by close and loving friends who bring their own brands of joy and laughter into our home. It is easy to forget sometimes that we are here because I can no longer get into their houses.

Debbie wrote in her brother's obituary how hard it must have been for him to watch all his friends die of AIDS, given how excruciating it is for her to watch one friend struggle with ALS. I don't often attend to how hard this must be on my close friends — how hard it would be for me to watch someone go through this and not be able to change the course. Humor and good spirits are what I can offer to make this easier on all of us. That, and inviting them to join me in howling at the moon.

You are invited to howl as well.

End of April/Indulge

MONDAY, APRIL 29, 2013

INDULGE

a : to give free rein to

b : to take unrestrained pleasure in : gratify

c : to yield to the desire of : humor <please indulge me
for a moment≥

d : to treat with excessive leniency, generosity, or con-
sideration

I have been very indulged lately, a word with a few
meanings. Spoiled, tolerated, humored, honored with

undue favor, forgiven. Some variations a little more obscure –

RC Church a remission of the temporal punishment for sin after its guilt has been forgiven

commerce an extension of time granted as a favor for payment of a debt or as fulfillment of some other obligation

Also called: Declaration of Indulgence a royal grant during the reigns of Charles II and James II of England giving Nonconformists and Roman Catholics a measure of religious freedom

Several years ago I attended Easter services at the Boston Cathedral of the Holy Cross in the city's South End. Cardinal Bernard Law was presiding, and this in the middle of the priest sex scandal. At one point during the service, he granted everyone in the church that day an "absolute indulgence". Not being Catholic, many of the rituals and dogma are lost on me. This is a particularly unusual one. As near as I can figure, all my sins up until that day in my life were forgiven. What a concept. Of course, it being mere chance that I was in the building that morning, I always assumed that the Cardinal was thinking more about his own sins than mine. But, even

Yes, Jesus does that every day, not the church. Because he died for us though I am not Catholic, I will take the gift of only having to concern myself with the sins of the last few years.

Imagine if we could all so easily offer each other an absolute indulgence. *Oh I wish I could tell you It's amazing, it's real*

But back to more realistic kinds of indulgences. *⟶ Not it is real*

1. indulge

2. [in-duhlj] Show IPA verb, in-dulged, in-dulg-ing.

3. verb (used without object)

4.1. to yield to an inclination or desire; allow oneself to follow one's will (often followed by in): Dessert came, but I didn't indulge. They indulged in unbelievable shopping sprees.

5. Verb (used with object)

6. 2. to yield to, satisfy, or gratify (desires, feelings, etc.): to indulge one's appetite for sweets. 3. to yield to the wishes or whims of; be lenient or permissive with: to indulge a child. 4. to allow (oneself) to follow one's will (usually followed by in): to indulge oneself in reckless spending. 5. Commerce to grant an extension of time,

for payment or performance, to (a person, company, etc.) or on (a bill, note, etc.).

I cannot possibly list all the ways my friends have spoiled me these last few months. Little indulgences like bringing a coffee latte, big indulgences like coming to spend the weekend armed with bags of food and tools to complete the chores I can no longer do. You hung bird feeders to distract my troubled thoughts, paid my bills, filled out forms and walked my silly dog. Those in the bbc (bare butt club) go the extra mile.

I am indulged by no longer having to wash dishes, make an occasional meal or fold laundry.

You also indulge my bad jokes, silly wheelchair races, my sad days and you indulge me this blog!

Now I have to ask for a very big indulgence – treat with excessive leniency. Please forgive in advance for being slow to answer the phone; it takes me longer to pick it up than there are rings. Please forgive me if I am slow to return your call, speaking gets sloppier as the day goes on. Please forgive my one word emails and text messages, it is getting harder to type on my phone and to lift my laptop to my lap and open the lid. And please don't stop writing, texting and calling, but understand that this disease saps my energy. I will do my very best to uphold my end of the conversation.

April News:

I lost the second great scooter wheel chair challenge race. Based on the time difference in the finish of the first race, we agreed to a 20 second head start for the scooter. Big Mistake! The scooter won by 8 seconds. So we are even in the best two out of three. Date for the final race to be determined.

Bombs. We were not at the finish line and we live two miles from the Watertown search area. Since I no longer work I was able to get up the hill to watch the marathon race through my neighborhood. But there was a cool breeze and we were not dressed for a long outing so we were home just as the bombs exploded. Boston is such a small town that it seems that everyone knows someone who ran, volunteered, rescued, suffered, searched or were searched. There were only two degrees of separation this time, too close for all of us.

Spring is here and finally afternoons with enough sun to coax out the leaves, the blossoms and me. We have had nice "walks" along the Charles, naps on the front porch and hours reading under the budding cherry crab tree in the yard.

What's Next?

I am struggling more and needing more help with daily changes in my abilities. A couple of people have asked me if I am afraid. I am afraid of being totally incapacitated, but not of dying. We are making plans now for what is coming on fast. I really thought that I would have more time. A year ago this week I started the process of finding a diagnosis for my increasing balance problem.

This next month starts with a first communion, a dinner for my health providers and a road trip to DC.

On Grace and Karma

SUNDAY, MAY 26, 2013

I had a notion of karma – thinking if I spent my life doing good I would "earn" good — build some good karma. Good karma would keep bad things from happening. Now I see it does not work that way. Bad things happen. Grace is the ability to take on the bad things well, and karma is the gift of having people around who love, care and help.

I Am So Done
with ALS

MONDAY, JUNE 10, 2013

I am so done with ALS

I am so done with this f*&^king ALS!!!!

I do not want to feel sorry for myself but I am really, really, really upset about losing the use of my hands. The middle finger on each hand and the pinky on my right hand are still strong enough to type and hit the button on my cell phone, but that is it. I can no longer sign my name.

I skipped the May blog because I was beginning to bore myself. A lot happened in May. In retrospect, the thing that matters is that Mike graduated from college. He looked so happy in his cap and gown, it was enough joy to fill the month.

I have been thinking about intimacy. Not sexual or romantic intimacy, but the full range of physical, emotional and dare I say spiritual intimacy we are often embarrassed by (in bare ass?). We undress in front of our sexual partners, our physicians and maybe strangers in the locker room, but most of us would not consider having someone routinely remove our clothes. A few special friends may know some of our fears, our secrets and maybe our prayers. But generally we guard these parts of ourselves well – some of us very well indeed.

Among the many choices we have when suddenly sick is whether or not to fire our personal sentries. These sentries are the tricks, diversions, dodges and distractions we use to keep the world at bay. Don't we need these sentries guarding our vulnerable selves more when we are ill? Isn't this the time to circle wagons? And how do you know who to let past the palace guards? (I imagine mine dressed rather like the Swiss guys in striped pantaloons that guard the Pope.)

I have told my psych sentries to stand down; I have yet to fire them. They are milling about in the corner in their purple and gold stripes, helmets off with an occasional cigarette passing between them. I might be able to fire them someday but for now they still keep a watchful eye and spring into action from time to time, like a dog energetically greeting the postal carrier. Even so, while they have been relaxing, intimacy has been happening by choice and by necessity.

Intimate Strangers.

By necessity, there are a whole lot more people in my life now. Most notable are the four women who come at different times and frequencies to care for my daily physical needs. These people bathe me, brush my teeth, wipe me, feed me, get me in and out of bed and dress and undress me. As each week passes they bore through rock-hard walls of my self-consciousness, shyness, embarrassment and grief to move in close enough to keep me clean and safe and I fight them at every turn mistaking pride for dignity.

There are those who care for me who have such a well-worn familiarity with this disease that they anticipate both my physical and spiritual needs before I can imagine going there. They prepare both me and the path in front of me.

There are medical providers who know the science and my body – how it is collapsing. Two or three have also seen some of how my heart has broken. And my psychologist helps sort out the feelings about impending death from those born in ancient losses. There are a couple with whom I discuss both heart and health and who will be trusted with making the final call.

What sets these relationships apart is their inequality. They are one-way caring and no matter if I wished it otherwise, they are not friends and I will not share in the details of their lives. I do not question the authenticity of their caring, nor do I think them impervious to my not so subtle attempts to ensure that they like me. No, these intimate strangers are exactly as they need to be so they are ready to care for who comes next. But with some I do wish we had met in a different way at a different time.

Lines Blur

Last weekend the high-energy foursome came down from New Hampshire and moved in for the weekend giving Joan a much-needed respite away. Fun, food, great humor and help with chores made for a full weekend. Seeing people once a month helps to mark the changes and I notice how dependent I am on them and how much more intimate physical care they have to do for me. I also notice how much work it has become for me to remain actively in a conversation. Among friends the sentries have had to go for coffee while membership in the bare butt club grows and dinner conversation includes a discussion of the pros and cons of going on a ventilator. Joshua fought the battle of Jericho and the walls came a tumbling down.

As things become more difficult I know that I will need to let more people past my resting palace guards. It is a balance and I hope I can still decide how much will be shared, and with whom. I think about who can come with me to appointments not just based on schedules and interests, but who knows me well enough to speak for me as my voice fails – who knows my fears as well as my comforts.

The Eyes Have It

This month's blog essay is being composed using a computer that I'm controlling with my eyes. Each letter is selected individually from an on-screen keyboard by staring at it for two seconds. Often, especially with common or simple words, a list pops up based on some algorithm that predicts my next word, saving seconds per line.

→ why? Biologically speaking, is that the case?

Why share this detail? Well, if you know me then you know I'm really into the technology of this. If you are new to my circle, then you can appreciate the amount of time it took to write this. The thing about eyes is that these muscles are supposed to survive ALS. So since I can no longer type with my hands, and speech is too slurred to use dragon dictate, my eyes have to take over.

All of this has me thinking about eyes. Why does ALS spare the eyes? Maybe they are just among the last things to fail. Along the way the eyes witness and record each change, each loss. Eyes don't feel, they don't interpret. They are conduits sending information to the brain and the heart, and transmitting out sparkles and tears. And now my eyes are fingers, moving with an incredible lack of grace across the new keyboard. They betray and burn me when they tear, a different kind of disappointment these days. As a child I was told "stop crying or I'll give you something to cry about". Now, thanks to medications, tears I have sting, discouraging any release or relief otherwise promised from a good cry.

My two hazel beadies have a lot of work ahead, but they can't hold a candle to the workload of my "third eye", the observer. The observer is watching me live and die with ALS, and curiously studying my reaction to each loss of function. The observer self is detached but not out of touch. The observer is keeping me sane.

I watch myself maneuvering the wheelchair in my shadow on the sidewalk. When did any of us ever seriously imagine we might find ourselves dependent on a machine like this to leave the house? Am I really concerned that a two year old stranger will be scared by the chair, or me? Yes. And I think of how my friends might also be afraid, and then I touch my own fears, which need to be further explored.

The third eye watched as I was strapped into the lift for the round trip to the bathroom. I am weary of this chore, it hurts and is embarrassing. I'm like a hawk watching each helper, each time, to make sure I'm safely loaded knowing I'm not ready to die but knowing that I cannot live this way. I still have tasks on my to do list. This starts the internal debate; mortality, other people's needs, logistics, and that damn 'to do' list. And I watch as I'm moved back into my wheelchair, and watch the news as if I have an exam.

I can no longer use any fingers, and my voice will soon be gone. If we need to talk, call soon. Stay in touch, your emails brighten my day, your stories, jokes and goings on pull me out of my head.

We got to the Cape last month, thanks to Gerri and Billy and the loan of their accessible house in Chatham. It was great to get out of Newton. It was wonderful to be on the Cape, watching the fog roll in and out and back in again. The seals were swimming close to the beach so there were no people willing to chance confusing a shark. Seagulls tried to steal our lunch Saturday, on

Sunday we celebrated Joan's brother's birthday on the porch of the Chatham Bars Inn, very swank.

This is a new phase of my illness, but a familiar place for those who know the well-worn path. If ALS were quicksand, I would be up to my neck! I am helpless, no intention to whine, but to simply say it, and I, the great introvert, can no longer be left alone. The good news is that there are friends to be with me in the gaps. The next decisions will be about a feeding tube to take over as my ability to swallow diminishes, and breathing support at least at night. More machines. I feel like no matter how proactive I am, the disease moves too fast for me and I cannot catch my breath. This eye operated computer is a loaner and I hope my insurance approves the purchase quickly, before I lose my voice altogether.

Diagnosed one year ago this week.

Sorting and Tossing

SATURDAY, SEPTEMBER 7, 2013

Last fall I started clearing out stuff. It began at work with old files, books and the other sorts of junk we find in our desks – sticky pads, pens, conference name badges each with a story – each to a pile on the table. We all do this with changes in offices or jobs. First I moved home along with my small pile of important papers that found a place on the already crowded study table. More stuff followed months later when my staff gave up hope that I would come back.

Next on the list were the closets. I started with great resolve: I was going to complete this task of sorting and tossing so that Joan would not have to do this 'later'. Best laid plans. My friend, Donna, came and we started with the deep first floor hall closet and each winter dress coat, parka, and rain coat we hauled out betrayed the secret I share with other optimistic fat people that one day the favorite jackets will once again fit. Three trash bags later and we relocated our dig to the closet in my study, a true tribute to unbending optimism. Four more garbage bags and two suit cases later we had sorted through three decades of 'ever hopeful', 'just in case', and 'you never know'. And we had more than a few good laughs over the "I can't believe you ever wore" bag. Off to Goodwill.

I got the drawers in the bureau sorted with the help of my home health aide but ran out of legs and heart before I got to my every day clothes closet, my shoes, camera gear, books, papers, photos and handmade treasures from Mike.

We all 'spring clean' and go deeper into our wardrobes when facing life's big moments. I was gently reminded by a friend responding to my last post that we are all facing death, although the details may differ. I just have time to chronicle mine and share my inner sorting and tossing.

So what is important to keep and when do I toss the rest? What holds me back, why the caution still at this late date? Joan and some friends have started in on my now overflowing study that has become the dumping ground as I continue to shrink out of the stuff of my old life or progress past yet another aid to walking, dressing, eating or writing. They have started throwing /giving things away. It has been six months since I last sat up there at my desk, I have forgotten what is there beyond my camera gear. It will all go, but shouldn't there be some ritual to this gutting? No. I'm too tired to expend energy on stuff.

My own work, while others respectfully haul down my trash, is the sorting and tossing of hurt feelings, regrets, unmet expectations, unrealistic standards, false values and hypocritical judgments. Not to fear, I'm not working on sainthood, just giving up on martyrdom. I lack the strength to carry this crap any further. If you are mad at me for something I did more than 30 days ago, too late, give it up. I have. Unfortunately I'm also pulling things out of my bucket list.

Wouldn't it be great if we could do the emotional sorting and tossing each Spring? Right next to the Goodwill trailer in the grocery store parking lot there would be the 'bad will' trailer for slights more than thirty days past due, we could clear out our deep closets where we save our resentments 'just in case', 'you never know'. Therapy would be so much more effective. *yes you can give it all to Jesus His arms are wide enough, he can carry it.*

There are things I cannot yet bring myself to let go of no matter that I can no longer hold them or use them, selling on Craig's list makes too much sense. They still speak to a dream I want to hang on to. Here also old slights that, like a tumor, are still being nourished, awaiting some surgical final sever of the umbilical.

This month I will continue to work with the loaner Tobii eye gaze computer while I wait for mine now that the insurance coverage was approved (shout out to John Costello). I need to start using it to speak for me as well.

Joan is organizing her team for an ALS bike fundraiser; you will hear from her so shake your piggy bank.

When Mike was little and Joan would be out for the evening, he and I would climb into the big bed and watch scary movies. Mike was home this week; there's still magic in traditions. Sorting and tossing is a process, traditions will be last to go.

We're Dying
Richard Parker

WEDNESDAY, OCTOBER 30, 2013

"We're Dying, Richard Parker."

I'm not trying to be melodramatic. We are all dying.

When I had to move downstairs at the end of last February I bought a large screen TV and hooked it up to the Apple device so I could stream movies from my iPad. The first movie in the queue was The Life of Pi. Even if you have read the book, you need to see the movie. It is visually stunning. I dragged everyone into my room to watch it on the giant screen and, as a result, I watched that movie multiple times.

I will save us both from a retelling of the whole tale, but the main characters are a teenager who has taken the name Pi, and a tiger who was mistakenly assigned the name Richard Parker. After months fighting each other for survival in a life raft adrift in the open Pacific, the two emaciated combatants surrender momentarily. Pi slides down on the bench with the cat and takes its giant head in his lap and apologizes, "We are dying, Richard Parker ."

The question the storyteller throws us at the end is whether or not the tiger was really on the raft or if Pi has made up the story to avoid owning those parts of himself that are discordant with his self perception but were nevertheless essential to his survival. The man-eating, fierce, selfish carnivore did the necessary things or forced Pi to do things at odds with his values, in order to stay alive. All these parts that Pi has managed to distance himself from are momentarily joined – We're dying Richard Parker. Did Pi change to survive? Do we all have an inner tiger? Or some other alter ego capable of holding the pieces of self we are not comfortable with?

Another movie comes to my wandering mind – in order to save New York City, the character is asked to think of a scary symbol to be the tangible target in an onslaught from a bunch of spirits run amok. In "Ghostbusters," the stand-in is the Stay Puff marshmallow man. People in my life have suggested that this archetype may be closer to my hidden nature than Pi's tiger – the classic "iron coated marshmallow". All the soft, gooey, sweet, vulnerable parts of me, those parts I chose not to own, would be in my life raft. I would be floating adrift with the Stay Puff marshmallow guy. Oh wait a minute, I AM in a life raft with a giant marshmallow! So, we're dying, marshmallow guy!!

A group of colleagues from my last job came to dinner at the end of September. The group included two friends from DC and one from the NYC office who all came into town to join the local staff to have dinner with me. I was not just touched, I was grabbed in a bear hug of appreciation that still has a hold on me. The weekend before, I spent with my good buddies from NH. The weekend after, 13 friends rode their bikes together after raising $16,000 for ALS research and advocacy. Another dozen friends waited at the ride's finish line for team "Holly's Heroes" to cross, all in their matching bright orange shirts. A week later, I was joined by 14 people coming in from DC, NJ, NY, Cape Cod and our local family to attend a fundraising dinner for the research organization ALSTDI.

It is now mid October and the NH gang is back. In between there have been countless afternoon visits, dinners and help getting me into bed. (And you wonder why this blog is late?)

I'm surrounded and humbled by love and support. I know I have written about this before, but I am blessed. I keep wondering when you all will get bored and go away. But that's just my insecure self rumbling. I'm not one who will ever write the book on what great things I learned from having ALS or the great joy of struggle and pain while basking in the silver lining of a terminal disease. This sucks and I cannot pretend for a second that it is anything less than a horrible way to die. But you, my friends, have made it easier, more gentle.

I am surprised by how much I have laughed this last year – much more than I ever have, and that includes laughing at myself. I have a greater appreciation for showers, car rides, take-out, dog walkers and, of course, vodka. Some of you suggest that I have changed – that the reason why I'm "feeling the love" is because I have somehow been renovated by this process. I don't think that's it. Rather I have, like Pi, sat down with my tiger's head in my lap and taken ownership of my full self. In so doing, giving the "softer" parts of myself equal time, I have not changed, I have revealed. Perhaps personal crises give us permission to be our full selves.

While enjoying my friends, I'm painfully aware how short my time with you is. It knocks me to my knees to think how I have squandered all of this for so many years. When I find myself in the pity pond thinking how much I will miss you, or the changing leaves, or Nantucket or movies with Mike – I remind myself that "missing", like wine and ice cream, is for the living.

Conversation is difficult. Talking, while still possible, depends on the time of day and often requires repeating each word. I'm also having more trouble sleeping, and that means Joan is not able to sleep through the night. I am saying goodbye to more of my favorite foods. While all these are extensively discussed in ALS patient guides, I really thought I might be able to avoid these symptoms. I have new machines to help me breathe and in a couple of weeks I will have surgery to put in a feeding tube.

But the Red Sox are in the World Series and I got to go to a game, Mike is home for a visit and the dog, while too big, is nevertheless curled up asleep in my lap. Today, all is right with the world.

Betrayal by Mouth

THURSDAY, DECEMBER 26, 2013

There is nothing creative or inspirational here. This is a lament. I failed to produce a blog entry for November. It is hard to be witty and creative when you are scared and feel like crap. Harder still when trying to convince yourself and all those around that everything is fine. November was a tough month.

I have been focused on my misbehaving mouth. We have all had the experience of being betrayed by our mouths. The taste of your foot familiar? Acquainted with the moment when your mouth wins and you are eating another cookie, your brain screaming nooo! And who can honestly say that nothing has ever fallen back out of your opened mouth – victim to a hearty but no less ill timed laugh. Don't pretend you haven't ever accidentally spit on someone and feigned not to be on speaking terms with your mouth.

Speaking about speaking, has your mouth started to betray you verbally? Your mind thinks oven, your mouth blurts 'fridge'? And secrets seem to just fall out like a five-year-old's teeth. You say what is on your mind and realize a split second later that you can't take it back and will never live it down. I'm reminded of a trip through customs; when asked if I had anything to declare my mouth replied "nothing but some Cuban cigars." My mouth then led the rest of me over to special line 6 while my mind worked quickly on a way out of the mess. Bite your tongue.

So on a good day we have to all watch our mouths. Mine now requires extraordinary surveillance. There is a war raging. My teeth have turned to the dark side attacking the inside of the cheeks at will. They fight against each other crashing and grinding through the night threatening to break, occasionally nipping my tongue – collateral damage. Medication dries it to death valley until a flash flood of spit overwhelms, a trademark of ALS.

I eat only food that my infant tongue can now safely convey from the front of my mouth to my throat. As with each muscle group and previous failed function, I'm keenly aware of the synchronization and complex interplay of muscles required for us to complete the simplest of activities, like eating. I think about how quickly I used to eat, only slowing down occasionally to savor a really fine meal. It is not a habit that I'm particularly fond of. On a trip to Thailand we visited a lotus farm and had lunch with the Buddhist teacher in his hut floating above the river. His instruction – chew each bite 40 times before you swallow. That will certainly slow you down! I no longer have this problem and avoid any food that could hold together past four chews.

In fact, I'm taking much of my nourishment now through a feeding tube that was put in during a procedure in November. Sparing the details, it is white, about the diameter of a thin drinking straw, and is located about 3 inches above my navel. I have what looks like an iv bag dripping a vanilla shake directly into my belly. I'm not sure why they wasted the effort flavoring the stuff since it comes nowhere near my taste buds.

The feeding tube came in November, not in response to my mouth but my diminishing breathing capacity and the relative risks of surgery. The window was closing. So off I went, but it was not smooth. I had a rough go of it.

Being asked the question we all think we are prepared for is a mind clarifying moment. I have been clear that when the time comes, I don't want to be kept alive on a ventilator. I want no heroic measures. Because my breathing capacity is now less than 30%, there was a risk that I would not be able to come off the respirator either right after surgery or at all. So when they couldn't take me off in recovery, they moved me to the ICU. Time came to try again about 20 hours later, and there were quiet confirmations at the foot of my bed of the DNR. Then my doctor asked me the question: if the extubation was unsuccessful, did I want them to re-intubate me and try again. The alternative was unspoken. Hell yes try again!

A few years ago, in the middle of the health care debate, there was a lot of conversation about so called "death panels". In recognition that often the last year of life is the most expensive, the proposal was to provide doctors and patients the opportunity to discuss options in end of life planning. I smugly considered myself immune to the irrational choice to toss good money after bad, to pull out all the stops with certain and inevitable outcomes. But I would make my stand against excessive medical care when I was 85 not 58.

I've had a change of heart. I still can't agree to life on a ventilator (but respect those who have made another choice); short of that, I'm greedy. I want every drug, every procedure and every treatment my doctor has to offer. Bar none. I want to live, lust for a chance to continue.

I am sure I'm not alone in my foxhole conversion. And the bill for the procedure and hospitalization exceeded the annual income of 97% of people in the world, a morality question for another blog. This is bad news for policy makers and budget planners. Patients like me won't behave rationally. But back to my mouth.

The worst part of the last month has been the departure of voice. I know I've been complaining about this for a while. But the moment has come when even I cannot understand the sounds coming out of my mouth. My brain is so clear about what needs to be said but my tongue can no longer form the words.

Each change this year shrinks my world. This change has been the biggest step in shrinking me.

My Dog Amuses Me

TUESDAY, JANUARY 28, 2014

It is January, snowy and bitterly cold. There are a few hopeful birds still showing up at the feeders, but they are empty. Walker enjoys watching them. My dog amuses me. He is an 8 year old beagle basset hound. He can't be left alone, so he has really enjoyed this last year with me at home. He assumes the bird feeders were hung on the tree outside the window for his amusement, and the placement of the large footstool under the window an invitation to his comfort. The fact that the windowsill is the perfect height for him to rest his chin is, of course, to be expected.

He takes advantage of everyone. His manners have hit an all time low. He behaves for Mike on occasion. Walker adores Mike. He is every inch a DOG.

When I recorded phrases last summer for the message bank, I included messages for him. "Come Walker, come," gets his attention. "You want a cookie" gets him every time, the combination of the familiar voice and the promise of a treat are too overwhelming a combination to ignore.

I started banking messages as my voice started failing. I wish I had started earlier, when my voice was strong. But that would have required me to accept the inevitable loss of speech much earlier as well. Instead, over the course of a couple of weeks, I recorded some 800 phrases ranging from generic "may I have..." to highly personal terms of endearment.

While we are still perfecting the setup, the phrases are loaded on my Tobii i-15 eye controlled computer and I'm able to select a phrase, or string a number of phrases together to drop into a conversation. The pleasure comes in seeing the reaction of others, including my dog, to the familiar sound. I am trying to incorporate these phrases into my regular use of the Tobii, at the same time I am calling on the Tobii to take over my total speech.

I miss easy conversation, I miss adding an opinion, offering a correction or supplying a missing word. I miss the wise crack, the pun and the punch line. I wish I had thought to record myself singing 'Happy Birthday to You'.

If wishes were horses then beggars would ride. It's January and Christmas is over and the tree is gone and decorations packed away. It doesn't feel like a new year, maybe because I have no new calendar.

Bring no more vodka, no more food. Just come now empty handed and with your always full hearts. Or maybe bring food and treats for each other. Joan likes Sancerre and flowers. I would hate for you to see what has be done to that beautiful flourless chocolate cake, the eggplant Parmesan, the meatloaf, so that I can eat it. Not even store-bought muffins deserve this treatment.

I'm swimming in vodka. You have been very generous. I am having trouble with things tasting too bitter, too tart. The vodka mixers are hard to handle. So I'm slowing down even here, and there are times now when I really need a drink! The same muscles that drive speech control swallowing.

I'm having a system-wide shutdown. We spend our lives practicing the art of living yet all the while we are tumbling toward death.

I find myself closer to the place and suddenly realize that I have no idea how to die. We never practice. When I was little we played cowboys and Indians, cops and robbers 'combat'. When you were shot you grabbed your chest, fell to the ground saying 'goodbye cruel world', rolled your head to the side and let your tongue hang out. As we got older and more sophisticated we dropped the 'goodbye cruel world' and sometimes had to wait for the designated medic to declare us dead before we could assume a new identity and continue playing.

That was a long time ago. I don't think those games will help me now. Yet as I think about dying, these games and the final moments of a couple of friends with AIDS, are as close as I have been to a dress rehearsal. And I do so want to get this right. I think I have a pretty good idea what happens physically, barring complications. I don't want to panic about not being able to breathe, so when the time comes I won't be stoic.

But the mind, imagination and emotions are a mystery to me. What churns as we die? Last night I dreamed I was playing golf, and as is common in all my dreams, I know I have ALS but I am not limited by it. I'm left wondering how I can be unable to move my head on the pillow but able to hit a pure seven iron on a par three.

The other night I dreamed I was in Peru and I was on a woody path following my brother and sister who had left me and had gone on ahead. The path came to an abrupt end at a packed church. Confused, I went inside. It was clear that I was not welcome. The people spoke a language unfamiliar to my ear, and I was unable to communicate. As they hustled me out a different door, and onto a new path, I managed to glance into the amazing sanctuary. Every one inside was in a circle dance. Each wore a tiger skin cloak, with several more skins hanging on pegs in the wall. As I left on my new path, I added tigers to the list of cautions and reminded myself I was walking.

Will dying be more dreams of exploring or playing golf in which I have failed to incorporate my paralyzed self, will my subconscious check out still believing that I can walk, talk and put on a tiger cloak?

We are talking to the hospice team again, still trying to sort out the insurance. They know how to die. Maybe I can practice with them. I have a fantasy. All my closest friends are here in my house with me. There is music and everyone is calm. But that means I can't die anytime soon.

Most of my friends are leaving on vacation for most of the next month. I am safe for February.

The News and Weather

TUESDAY, APRIL 8, 2014

Okay, I know it has been a long time since my last blog post. I have been busy. Well, maybe not so much busy as in transition. That my health continues to slide isn't a surprise, what does surprise me is how the human spirit can continue to adjust to change.

Joan's brother Ed died at the end of January. His heart was supposed to outlast me. It did not. The earth shifted. And our spirits must adjust to the void. He was my brother-in-love if not in-law.

I'm discovering that you can make do without a voice. It is not possible to have intimate, deeply personal or meaningful conversations; for that you need time. These conversations cannot be mediator interpreted; they end up being all news and no weather, no nuance. Better now done through writing.

Mike moved back from New York. He just moved into an apartment in Watertown, a few miles away. It is great to have him here. He helps get me out of bed in the morning. Walker loves seeing him every day.

I just read on Facebook that Randy died at the end of last week. I never met him, but we were Facebook friends. He had a feeding tube procedure about two months after I had the same procedure. His did not go well, and he had to go back in a couple of times. He wrote and told me that he was depressed. Walter died earlier this year. He and I served on a committee together. After my last blog post he wrote to urge me to reconsider my decision not to have a ventilator. Maybe it is better not to know anyone else with ALS. That is probably not the right answer either.

I'm using my bi-pap machine almost all the time now. It's a breathing assist that increases the air I inhale and helps me exhale. This is for my failing diaphragm. It makes writing harder, the computer has trouble finding my eyes. I pretend the mask will keep cold germs away.

I have been thinking about Passover. Every year we join a large group at Janet and Irle's home for the Seder. It took a few years to figure out this feast was more about talking than eating, and we should give Mike dinner first, a few more to allow ourselves dinner first as well. Every one piles into a room with a large make-shift table a few inches above the floor with the expectation that we will all sit on the floor. Paul and I would scramble to get two seats together on the only couch in the room (yes, we pushed older people out of our way with no sense of shame). When one of the many wine bottles passed by us we snatched it and squirreled it and didn't share beyond a chosen few. We gossiped through the reading of the Haggadah until it was our time to read, surprising even ourselves that we knew where we were in the script. Then came the favorite part, the plagues: frogs, pestilence, boils, lice, locust, water to blood, death of the first born, etc. And to spare yourself, a secret code, blood of a lamb, or was it goat, smeared on your door?

I remember one conversation with an ALS clinic nurse and she said not everyone with ALS will get all the symptoms, not every Egyptian will suffer all the plagues.

Whose blood could I paint on my door? I feared losing my voice but on top of the plagues of losing my ability to walk, to write, to hold, to dress, to move, to eat, to drink, to speak, now I drool like a rabid bull dog. I got all the plagues.

Al Jazeera TV was here recently. They are doing a story on message banking, the pre-recorded phrases that I have on my computer, thanks to John Costello, that remind us all what my voice sounded like last summer. Every one performed well for the cameras, including Walker. It has been a long cold winter, but the light is back and there is, as always, the promise of spring. I'm still here. For now. I have not been out nor have I left the house since my hospital experience in November. In part it has just been too cold. In defense of my hibernation, my neck is growing too weak to operate the head controlled wheel chair. But I confess to laziness and apprehension, and that I have enough challenges in the house. I'm hoping to be here when the days are once again warm enough to allow me to sit in a sunspot on the porch. I think that I will feel less like I'm dying if I get my air fresh.

'Tis the new season, time for Fat Tuesday, Lent, Passover and Easter. Those who know Joan, know our house has decorations for every season, and I'm not talking a few knickknacks. No – we have bins full of stuff. We change pictures on the walls, cushions on the couches, not to mention the twenty or so stuffed bunnies that confuse the hell out of our rabbit hunting dog.

Fair to say that I can't keep up with the goal of a once a month essay. Let's agree to meet here every so often instead.

Next Chapter

MONDAY, MAY 12, 2014

It was 21 months ago that Holly received her official ALS diagnosis. It's been 21 months filled with blogs, advocacy, scooter and wheelchair races, love and support wide and big enough to fill Fenway Park, a clinical trial, potato vodka, movie days and dates with special friends, Mike's graduation and ultimate return to Boston as a core part of Holly's care team, profound personal loss for our family around the death of my brother, visits from far away colleagues, an intimate relationship with the Tobii computer, a published story in Cognoscenti, participation in an Al Jazeera Tech Know show on message banking and connections across all of the stages and phases of her remarkable life. Holly's "voice" continues to be loud via alphabet charts where, in very few words, she hits the nail on the head in vintage Holly style!

The Hospice team has now entered our lives to help us navigate this next chapter. Holly has, we think, the best caregiver team in America – from her Mass General ALS team to her beyond belief amazing PCP to her daily home health staff. They are blessings all. That said, you might appreciate one of her latest comments via the alphabet chart when she wanted "tangible solutions, not comfort" from us all! OK – we're on it!

Holly likely wrote her last blog a couple of weeks ago. Even though she is having a hard time writing, she can use the Tobii to read email which is now how she stays connected to her community of friends and extended family. Keep the email coming – hladd@rcn.com – you will likely not get a response but know it is read and treasured.

Be well and enjoy spring.

Joan

Epilogue

Holly Ladd died of ALS at her home on Monday, June 23rd, 2014. She was 59 years old.

That spring, we'd been told Holly had only a few days to live; she lived for another seven weeks. What she did during those final weeks of her life was a reflection of how Holly lived the 21 months since her diagnosis: a more intense version of her last 35 years.

She was driven to achieve goals.......she had a razor sharp focus......she fought hard for what she wanted....and she didn't waste time on what didn't matter. She wanted to milk every last drop out of this beautiful thing called life. What motivated her to stay with us for some extra time?

- She didn't want to "screw up" Mother's Day

- She wanted to be around for her brother David's visit on his return from a trip to Canada

- She didn't want to interfere with our niece Catherine's graduation from Holy Cross College

- She wanted to stick around for the family's annual golf tournament on Cape Cod even though she hadn't played in two years, and

- She wanted to make it to Mike's 24th birthday on June 10th

As long as her eye muscles held out, Holly could be part of the world. She could use her alphabet charts to make her needs known, to tease those of us in her path, to guide us through set ups of various digital devices, to laugh, and to use her Tobii computer to connect and to contribute. She loved to be "of use."

In the <u>Boston Globe</u> obituary on June 25th, Holly was described this way: "Always ready to venture beyond her comfort zone, Holly may be hopping on a small airplane to fly to a tiny air strip in rural Kenya, or boarding a jet to fly to Oklahoma in the wake of a devastating tornado. Holly took joy in helping others throughout her life."

Holly was cremated and her ashes were buried in Newton Cemetery next to a small pond and waterfall with her favorite hydrangeas nearby. Her grave marker sports a camera etched into the granite to reflect her retirement plan of portrait photography.

More than two hundred of Holly's friends and family were present at her Memorial Service where people spoke, read poems, sang pieces Holly had requested, and reflected with humor and wisdom on her amazing life. Our son, Mike, read the following short poem.

"Death Stands By"
By Bert Stiles

Climbers, true climbers, are the strangest of men
Their love of the jagged peaks is so intense that it is
almost a religion
The boy loved climbing and had gone out the best way
Climbing that old scarred peak
We said nothing
But I soon found myself praying
That I, too, might die doing the thing I loved most.

Last November, when most of my communication with Holly was already email based, I asked her via email how she wanted to be remembered. She emailed the following answer on November 23, 2013:

"To be an idealist without illusions...to be a good friend....to live on the right side of history....to be someone who inspired action.....to be a good parent."

All agreed that she succeeded.

ACKNOWLEDGEMENTS

Much in the way that Holly's care called for a team of angels who arrived with wide wings, so too her blogs called for a savvy, artistic and compassionate team to produce this book.

Much gratitude to Judy Stoia, a dear friend of Holly's and now mine, for her time and effort in keeping the production moving forward with multiple re-writes and in locating the talent we needed to tackle the challenge of editing the book and designing the front and back covers; Abigail Strom for her clerk-of-the-works take charge role and sharp eye as the editor-in-chief of this venture----she gave countless hours and did much hand holding along the way; Jessica Tanny whose creative eye resulted in the cover designs which aptly convey Holly's spirit; Maggie Barmack for drafting and reading the text at an early stage and delivering a critique which enhanced the final work; Elissa Ely, a columnist and psychiatrist, for capturing so much of Holly's essence on

WBUR's "Remembrance Project" which now serves as the book's Introduction; to Ellie Sullivan and MaryEllen Mikula for their painstaking proofreading of the final text before sending to print; to Catherine Mikula for creating the layout for the book launch invitation on very short notice; to Laura Foti for bringing her tech skills to bear in creating the invitation; and to Holly's close personal friend, Donna Jeffers, for bringing her fundraising talents forward in hosting a charity book launch on September 10, 2015 to benefit The Augmentative Communication Program at Boston Children's Hospital.

What Holly received from John Costello and the Augmentative Communication Program brought quality and communication into her last year of life. She was on a quest to find ongoing support for it----the fundraiser was a step in that direction.

Ongoing and forever gratitude to Holly's team of friends, family and caregivers who show up as characters in her blogs and who helped to make her last two years one for the record books.

ABOUT THE AUTHOR

Holly Ladd was a lawyer with a lifetime involvement in civil rights and public health care, both in the U.S. and internationally. She lived in Newton, Massachusetts with her partner of twenty-five years and their twenty-four-year-old son. Diagnosed with ALS in 2012, her life work of advocacy in public policy took on a new dimension as she used her writing acumen to chronicle her journey of living and dying with this fatal condition.

34678487R00065

Made in the USA
Middletown, DE
30 August 2016